To

Kathryn

From

Laura

Gardener's
Book
of WISDOM

Walnut Grove Press
Nashville, TN 37202

The quoted ideas expressed in this book (but not scripture verses) are not, in all cases, exact quotations, as some have been edited for clarity and brevity. In all cases, the author has attempted to maintain the speaker's original intent. In some cases, quoted material for this book was obtained from secondary sources, primarily print media. While every effort was made to ensure the accuracy of these sources, the accuracy cannot be guaranteed. For additions, deletions, corrections or clarifications in future editions of this text, please write WALNUT GROVE PRESS.

Cover Design by Kim Russell / Wahoo Designs
Page Layout by Bart Dawson

ISBN 1-58334-266-4

Printed in the United States of America

Gardener's Book of WISDOM

Table of Contents

God almighty
first planted a garden.
And, indeed, it is among
the purest of human pleasures.

Francis Bacon

Introduction

Whenever we pause to consider God's glorious universe, we marvel at the miracle of nature. The smallest seedlings and grandest stars are all part of God's infinite creation. God has placed His handiwork on display for all to see, and if we're wise, we make time each day to celebrate the world that surrounds us.

In the garden, we come face-to-face, nose-to-nose, and hand-to-hand with God's good earth. Thus, the garden is a perfect place to observe the Creator's work and to sense His presence.

This book celebrates the pleasures, the joys, and the lessons of gardening. The text also includes Bible verses and quotations that celebrate the glory of God's creation *and* the miracle of His unending love.

Success in the garden—or outside it—depends upon certain unchanging principles. So, if you're ready to get your hands dirty and dig for insights about land and life, turn the page. But before you do, give thanks to your Creator for *all* the opportunities He has given you—including, of course, the opportunity to tend a garden.

God's Creation

And to every beast of the earth and to every bird of the sky
and to every thing that moves on the earth which has life . . .
God saw all that He had made, and behold, it was very good.

Genesis 1:30-31 NASB

The observant gardener witnesses a show like no other. And the price of admission is indeed a bargain: a plot of ground, a ray of hope, and a handful of seeds.

Today presents another opportunity to celebrate God's handiwork. Will you join in the celebration? If you are wise, you will pause and examine the exquisite details of God's glorious creation. When you do, you'll discover that the more carefully you inspect God's unfolding universe, the more beautiful it becomes.

Sometimes, a garden can be a frustrating place. Plants can be stubborn, pests can be persistent, and weather can be uncooperative. When things begin to grow wrong, so do emotions—but no one should work the soil in anger (especially you!)

So the next time you find yourself muttering about weeds, weather, or bugs, pause to give thanks for your garden; it's a gift from God that keeps on giving—and as a gardener, you're strongly advised to keep on *thanking* Him for that gift.

No philosophical theory which I have yet come across
is a radical improvement on the words of Genesis,
that "in the beginning God made Heaven and Earth."

C. S. Lewis

To create a little flower is the labor of ages.

William Blake

It is impossible to account for the creation of the universe without the agency of a Supreme Being. It is impossible to govern the universe without the aid of a Supreme Being. It is impossible to reason without arriving at a Supreme Being.

George Washington

Everything God does will remain forever;
there is nothing to add to it and there is nothing to take from it.

Ecclesiastes 3:14 NASB

God writes the gospel not in the Bible alone,
but on the trees, and flowers, and clouds, and stars.

Martin Luther

God and Nature first made us what we are,
and then out of our own created genius we make
ourselves what we want to be. Follow always that great law.
Let the sky and God be our limit and
Eternity our measurement.

Marcus Garvey

Big Bang theory—God Spoke and "Bang!"—It happened.

Anonymous

Then God saw everything that He had made,
and indeed it was very good.

Genesis 1:31 NKJV

Today, you will encounter God's creation.
When you see the beauty around you,
let each detail remind you to lift your head in praise.

Max Lucado

God is the beyond in the midst of our life.

Dietrich Bonhoeffer

The greatness of His power to create and design and form and mold and make and build and arrange defies the limits of our imagination. And since He created everything, there is nothing beyond His power to fix or mend or heal or restore.

Anne Graham Lotz

"Fear God and give Him glory, because the hour of
His judgment has come. Worship the Maker of heaven and earth,
the sea and springs of water."

Revelation 14:7 HCSB

Listen to the sermon preached to you by the flowers, the trees, the shrubs, the sky, and the whole world. Notice how they preach to you a sermon full of love, of praise of God, and how they invite you to glorify the sublimity of that sovereign Artist who has given them being.

Paul of the Cross

It is great—and there is no other greatness—to make one nook of God's creation more fruitful.

Thomas Carlyle

When God scooped out the valleys and created the mountains, when He hung the stars and blew the wind, you were on His mind.

Steve Brown

I will lift up my eyes to the hills—From whence comes my help? My help comes from the LORD, Who made heaven and earth.

Psalm 121:1-2 NKJV

God is an artist, and the universe is His work of art.

Thomas Aquinas

Beauty may be said to be God's trademark in creation.

Henry Ward Beecher

The God who created and numbers the stars in the heavens also numbers the hairs of my head. He pays attention to very big things and to very small ones. What matters to me matters to Him, and that changes my life.

Elisabeth Elliot

Do you not know? Have you not heard? The Everlasting God, the LORD, the Creator of the ends of the earth does not become weary or tired. His understanding is inscrutable. He gives strength to the weary, and to him who lacks might He increases power. Though youths grow weary and tired, and vigorous young men stumble badly, yet those who wait for the LORD will gain new strength; they will mount up with wings like eagles, they will run and not get tired, they will walk and not become weary.

Isaiah 40:28-31 NASB

How awesome that the "Word" that was in the beginning,
by which and through which God created everything,
was—and is—a living Person with a mind,
will, emotions, and intellect.

Anne Graham Lotz

It may be true time began in a garden.
It's time the way God created it: as servant, not master.

Emilie Barnes

He upholds the whole creation, founded the earth,
and still sustains it by the word of his power.
What cannot he do in the affairs of families and kingdoms,
far beyond our conception and expectation,
who hangs the earth upon nothing?

Matthew Henry

The LORD reigns; Let the earth rejoice.

Psalm 97:1 NKJV

God expresses His love through creation.

Charles Stanley

When we who have a feeling for birds observe
a mighty eagle, or the perfection of a tiny warbler, we see,
not the inspiration of God filtered through human agency,
but the very handiwork of the Creator Himself.

Rosalie Edge

The Lord God of heaven and earth, the Almighty Creator of
all things, He who holds the universe in His hand
as though it were a very little thing, He is your Shepherd,
and He has charged Himself with the care and
keeping of you, as a shepherd is charged
with the care and keeping of his sheep.

Hannah Whitall Smith

Those who wait upon the Lord, they shall inherit the earth.

Psalm 37:9 KJV

Go outside, to the fields, enjoy nature and the sunshine, go out and try to recapture happiness in yourself and in God. Think of all the beauty that's still left in and around you and be happy!

Anne Frank

What nature delivers to us is never stale, because what nature creates has eternity in it.

Isaac Bashevis Singer

We do not understand the intricate pattern of the stars in their course, but we know that He who created them does, and that just as surely as He guides them, He is charting a safe course for us.

Billy Graham

The heavens declare the glory of God; and the firmament shows His handiwork.

Psalm 19:1 NKJV

The world, space, and all visible components reverberate with God's Presence and demonstrate His Mighty Power.

Franklin Graham

Love all God's creation, both the whole and every grain of sand. Love every leaf, every ray of light. Love the animals, love the plants, love each separate thing. If thou love each thing thou will perceive the mystery of God in all.

Fyodor Dostoevsky

There is something incredibly comforting about knowing that the Creator is in control of your life.

Lisa Whelchel

Therefore if anyone is in Christ, he is a new creature; the old things passed away; behold, new things have come.

2 Corinthians 5:17 NCSB

Nature is too thin a screen; the glory of
the omnipresent God bursts through everywhere.

Ralph Waldo Emerson

Let every Christian be a gardener so that he and she and
the whole creation which groans in expectation of
the Spirit's final harvest, may inherit paradise.

Vigen Guroian

All the power of God—the same power that hung the stars
in place and put the planets in their courses and
transformed Earth—now resides in you to energize and
strengthen you to become the person God created you to be.

Anne Graham Lotz

God lifted him high and honored him far beyond anyone or
anything, ever, so that all created beings in heaven and earth,
even those long ago dead and buried, will bow in worship before this
Jesus Christ, and call out in praise that he is the Master of all,
to the glorious honor of God the Father.

Philippians 2:9-11 MSG

Nature, as a whole and in all its elements,
enunciates something that may be regarded as
an indirect self-communication of God to all those
ready to receive it.

Martin Buber

A garden teems with life. It glows with color and
smells like heaven and puts forward at every hour of
a summer day beauties which man could never have created
and could not even, on his own resources, have imagined.

C. S. Lewis

Thoreau declared, "In wildness is the preservation of
the world." I believe that in wildness is the preservation
of the soul. More than ever, we need to seek out a renewal
of our spirits from the Creator's ultimate manifest source.
Nature alone has always been regarded by all peoples
as an authentic cache of the Holy.

F. Lynne Bachleda

He is the image of the invisible God, the firstborn over all creation;
because by Him everything was created, in heaven and on earth,
the visible and the invisible, whether thrones or dominions or rulers
or authorities—all things have been created through Him and for Him.

Colossians 1:15 HCSB

A Gardener's Prayer

Dear Lord, You have created a world that is glorious
to behold yet impossible to comprehend.
I praise You for Your creation, Father, and for the sense
of awe and wonder that You have placed in my heart.
Today, as I venture out to my garden,
I will pause to admire Your handiwork.
This is the day that You have made,
and I will rejoice in it.
Amen

The Joys of Gardening

The LORD is king! Let the earth rejoice!
Let the farthest islands be glad.

Psalm 97:1 NLT

Gardening, if done properly, is a joyful pursuit. Whether it's a big two-acre spread or a tiny midtown window box, a garden is a place where the majesty of nature is revealed each day.

As the seasons pass and the cycle of life unfolds, thoughtful gardeners (like you) pause to reflect upon the infinite power of the Creator and the infinite value of His creation.

Joy, whether in the garden or outside it, is a choice. How will *you* choose?

C. H. Spurgeon, the renowned 19th-century English clergyman, could have been talking about a *garden* gate when he advised, "The Lord is glad to open the gate to every knocking soul. It opens very freely; its hinges are not rusted; no bolts secure it. Have faith and enter at this moment through holy courage. If you knock with a heavy heart, you shall yet sing with joy of spirit. Never be discouraged!"

If, today, your heart is heavy, open the door of your soul to Christ. He will give you peace and joy. And, if you already have the joy of Christ in your heart, share it freely, just as Christ freely shared His joy with you.

The joy of anything, from a blade of grass upwards,
is to fulfill its created purpose.

Oswald Chambers

How fair is a garden amid the toils and passions of existence.

Benjamin Disraeli

Gardening has compensations out of all proportion
to its goals. It is creation in the pure sense.

Phyllis McGinley

I will thank you, LORD, with all my heart;
I will tell of all the marvelous things you have done.
I will be filled with joy because of you.
I will sing praises to your name, O Most High.

Psalm 9:1-2 NLT

A thing of beauty is a joy forever:
Its loveliness increases . . . .

John Keats

What I enjoy is not the fruits alone,
but I also enjoy the soil itself.

Cicero

The essence of the enjoyment of a garden is that
things should look as though they like to grow in it.

Beatrix Farrand

Make me hear joy and gladness.

Psalm 51:8 NKJV

All of us tend to put off living. We are all dreaming of some magical rose garden over the horizon instead of enjoying the roses that are blooming outside our windows today.

Dale Carnegie

The lesson I have thoroughly learnt, and wish to pass on to others, is to know the enduring happiness that the love of a garden gives.

Gertrude Jekyll

Say your prayers in a garden early, ignoring steadfastly the dew, the birds and the flowers, and you will come away overwhelmed by its freshness and joy; go there in order to be overwhelmed.

C. S. Lewis

Delight yourself also in the LORD,
and He shall give you the desires of your heart.

Psalm 37:4 NKJV

Deciding what to grow is one of the most enjoyable aspects of gardening.

Burpee Complete Gardener

The greatest gift of a garden is the restoration of the five senses.

Hanna Rion

So, if you cannot understand that there is something in man which responds to the challenge of this mountain and goes out to meet it, that the struggle is the struggle of life itself upward and forever upward, then you won't see why we go. What we get from this adventure is just sheer joy.

Sir George Mallory

You will show me the way of life, granting me the joy of your presence and the pleasures of living with you forever.

Psalm 16:11 NLT

Working in the garden gives me something beyond
the enjoyment of the senses.
It gives me a profound feeling of inner peace.

Ruth Stout

One should learn also to enjoy the neighbor's garden,
however small; the roses straggling over the fence,
the scent of lilacs drifting across the road.

Henry Van Dyke

I should like to enjoy this summer flower by flower,
as if it were to be the last one for me.

André Gide

Rejoice evermore. Pray without ceasing.
In every thing give thanks: for this is the will of God
in Christ Jesus concerning you.

1 Thessalonians 5:16-18 KJV

Deviation from Nature is deviation from happiness.

Samuel Johnson

Every gardener knows that one of the chief joys of
his activity is working deeply with the soil,
pushing one's hands deep into its moist,
life-giving crumbliness.

Jeff Cox

Oh, this is the joy of the rose—that it blooms and goes.

Willa Cather

This is the day the LORD has made; let us rejoice and be glad in it.

Psalm 118:24 NIV

He who plants a garden plants happiness.

Anonymous

It's difficult to think anything but pleasant thoughts
while eating a homegrown tomato.

Lewis Grizzard

Health, wealth, and happiness will come forth
from the earth if we diligently work for the harvest.

Jim G. Brown

Shout with joy to the LORD, O earth! Worship the LORD with gladness.
Come before him, singing with joy.

Psalm 100:1-2 NLT

A Gardener's Prayer

Dear Lord, when I am working in the garden—
and when I am not—I will choose to be
a joyful Christian. You have given me countless
blessings, and I will celebrate Your gifts.
I will make Your joy my joy. I will praise Your works,
I will obey Your Word, and I will honor Your Son,
this day and every day of my life.
Amen

Attitude

When a man is gloomy, everything seems to go wrong;
when he is cheerful, everything seems right!

Proverbs 15:15 TLB

The gardener's life should be cause for celebration, but sometimes we don't feel much like celebrating. In fact, when the weight of the world seems to bear down upon our shoulders, celebration may be the last thing on our minds . . . but it shouldn't be. As God's children, we are all blessed beyond measure on good days and bad. This day is a non-renewable resource—once it's gone, it's gone forever. We should give thanks for this day while using it for the glory of God.

What will be your attitude today? Will you be fearful, angry, bored, or worried? Will you be cynical, bitter or pessimistic? If so, God wants to have a little talk with you.

God created you in His own image, and He wants you to experience joy and abundance. But, God will not force His joy upon you; you must claim it for yourself. So today, and every day hereafter, celebrate the life that God has given you. Think optimistically about yourself and your future. Give thanks to the One who has given you everything, and trust in your heart that He wants to give you so much more.

We can complain because rose bushes have thorns,
or rejoice because thorn bushes have roses.

Abraham Lincoln

Eventually, a gardener becomes a philosopher.

Barbara Dodge Borland

The fair-weather gardener, who will do nothing except when the wind and weather and everything else are favorable, is never a master of his craft.

Henry Ellacombe

Keep your eyes focused on what is right,
and look straight ahead to what is good.

Proverbs 4:25 NCV

Good thoughts bear good fruit and bad thoughts bear bad fruit. And a man is his own gardener.

James Allen

The man who has planted a garden feels that he has done something for the good of the whole world.

Charles Dudley Warner

Climate is the single-most important factor in how plants grow—indeed in what we select to plant in the first place.

Jack Kramer

Finally, brothers, whatever is true, whatever is noble, whatever is right, whatever is pure, whatever is lovely, whatever is admirable–if anything is excellent or praiseworthy–think about such things.

Philippians 4:8 NIV

Flowers always make people better, happier,
and more helpful; they are sunshine,
food and medicine for the soul.

Luther Burbank

Nature and the garden bring out the best in our characters.

Felicity Bryan

Growing a garden and staying out in the fresh air
after office hours seemed to give me the strength
to meet all problems with greater courage.

Jim G. Brown

Your attitude should be the same that Christ Jesus had.

Philippians 2:5 NLT

Earth laughs in flowers.

Ralph Waldo Emerson

As is the garden such is the gardener.
A man's nature runs either to herbs or weeds.

Francis Bacon

Gardening is a labor full of tranquility and satisfaction;
natural and instructive, and as such contributes
to the most serious contemplation,
experience, health and longevity.

John Evelyn

For the word of God is living and active.
Sharper than any double-edged sword, it penetrates
even to dividing soul and spirit, joints and marrow;
it judges the thoughts and attitudes of the heart.

Hebrews 4:12 NIV

There is no spot of ground, however arid,
bare, or ugly, that cannot be tamed.

Gertrude Jekyll

Cares melt when you kneel in your garden.

Anonymous

There is something about sun and soil
that heals broken bodies and jangled nerves.

Nature Magazine

You were taught, with regard to your former way of life,
to put off your old self, which is being corrupted by its
deceitful desires; to be made new in the attitude of your minds;
and to put on the new self, created to be like God
in true righteousness and holiness.

Ephesians 4:22-24 NIV

A Gardener's Prayer

Dear Lord, help me have an attitude that is pleasing to You as I count my blessings today, tomorrow, and every day of my life. Whatever this day may hold—and whatever the harvest may be—let my response reflect a God-honoring attitude of optimism, faith, and love for You.
Amen

Peace

The LORD bless you and keep you;
The LORD lift His countenance upon you, and give you peace.

Based on Numbers 6:24-26

One of the most important crops from any garden can—and should—be the feeling of peace that grows in the gardener's heart. That sense of peace is most readily achieved in silence.

Silence is among the most endearing qualities of a garden. When, in the quiet early morning hours, we sink our hands into God's good earth, all is right with the world.

Elisabeth Elliot made a statement and followed it with a question; she said, "The world is full of noise. Might we not set ourselves to learn silence, stillness, solitude?" The answer, of course, is that we *should* avail ourselves of the wisdom that comes from silence and solitude—but all too often, we don't.

The next time you visit your chosen patch of soil, be still and listen to the gentle sounds of nature. You'll be glad you did because a quiet garden is guaranteed to restore your perspective and nourish your soul.

I have never been happier, more exhilarated,
at peace, inspired, and aware of the grandeur of
the universe and greatness of God than
when I find myself in a natural setting
not much changed from the way He made it.

Jimmy Carter

Silence is a great peacemaker.

Henry Wadsworth Longfellow

Flowers and plants are silent presences;
they nourish every sense but the ear.

Mary Sarton

God has called us to live in peace.

1 Corinthians 7:15 NIV

Climb the mountains and get their good tidings.
Nature's peace will flow into you as sunshine flows into trees. The winds will blow their own freshness into you, and the storms their energy, while cares drop off the autumn leaves.

John Muir

God is the friend of silence.
Trees, flowers, grass grow in silence.
See the stars, moon, and sun, how they move in silence.

Mother Teresa

Christ alone can bring lasting peace—
peace with God—peace among men and nations—
and peace within our hearts.

Billy Graham

Live peaceful and quiet lives in all godliness and holiness.

1 Timothy 2:2 NIV

My good hoe as it bites the ground revenges my wrongs,
and I have less desire to bite my enemies.
In smoothing the rough hillocks, I smooth my temper.

Ralph Waldo Emerson

No matter how sophisticated you may be, a large granite mountain cannot be denied—it speaks in silence to the very core of your being. There are some that care not to listen but the disciples are drawn to the high altar with magnetic certainty, knowing that a great Presence hovers over the ranges.

Ansel Adams

Peace does not mean to be in a place where there is no noise, trouble, or hard work. Peace means to be in the midst of all those things and still be calm in your heart.

Catherine Marshall

And the peace of God, which transcends all understanding, will guard your hearts and your minds in Christ Jesus.

Philippians 4:7 NIV

To know one's landscape, to feel in sympathy with it,
is often to be at peace with life. When all the world seems
wrong and the burdens overwhelming he can look out on
the familiar fields and hills or get among them and
give way to their beauties of form and color as
a resource within himself that will be
an everpresent power of recuperation.

Richard E. Dodge

Arranging a bowl of flowers in the morning can give
a sense of quiet in a crowded day—
like writing a poem or saying a prayer.

Anne Morrow Lindbergh

When peace like a river attendeth my way,
When sorrows like sea billows roll;
Whatever my lot, Thou hast taught me to say,
"It is well, it is well with my soul."

Horatio G. Spafford

Blessed are the peacemakers, for they shall be called sons of God.

Matthew 5:9 NKJV

Rest is not idleness, and to lie sometimes on the grass on a summer day listening to the murmur of the water, or watching the clouds float across the sky, is hardly a waste of time.

John Lubbock

Quiet places should be enjoyed. Save the quiet places first.

Ernest Lyons

Christ is not only a remedy for your weariness and trouble, but he will give you an abundance of the contrary: joy and delight. They who come to Christ do not only come to a resting-place after they have been wandering in a wilderness, but they come to a banqueting-house where they may rest, and where they may feast. They may cease from their former troubles and toils, and they may enter upon a course of delights and spiritual joys.

Jonathan Edwards

Come to Me, all you who are weary and burdened, and I will give you rest. Take My yoke upon you and learn from Me, because I am gentle and humble in heart, and you will find rest for your souls. For My yoke is easy and My burden is light.

Matthew 11:28-30 HCSB

A garden is meant ro be a place of spiritual repose, stillness, peace, refreshment, and delight.

John Henry Cardinal Newman

Man is happy in a garden because God has made him so and to live in a garden is the nearest he can reach to paradise on earth.

Nan Fairbrother

Are you weak? Weary? Confused? Troubled? Pressured?
How is your relationship with God?
Is it held in its place of priority?
I believe the greater the pressure,
the greater your need for time alone with Him.

Kay Arthur

I wait quietly before God, for my salvation comes from him.

Psalm 62:1 NLT

The silence of nature is very real. It surrounds you.
You can feel it.

Ted Trueblood

We may have to learn again the mystery of the garden: how its external characteristics model the heart itself, and how the soul is a garden enclosed, our own perpetual paradise where we can be refreshed and restored.

Thomas More

We Christians must simplify our lives or lose untold treasures on earth and in eternity. Modern civilization is so complex as to make the devotional life all but impossible. The need for solitude and quietness was never greater than it is today.

A. W. Tozer

And he withdrew himself into the wilderness, and prayed.

Luke 5:16 KJV

A Gardener's Prayer

Dear Lord, in the quiet moments of this day,
I will turn my thoughts and prayers to You.
In silence I will sense Your presence, and I will seek
Your will for my life, knowing that when I accept
Your peace, I will be blessed today
and throughout eternity.
Amen

Planning

The plans of the diligent lead to profit as surely as haste leads to poverty.

Proverbs 21:5 NIV

"Plan your work, then work your plan" is a bit of advice we have all heard over and over. But reminders about the importance of planning are always worth repeating, especially to gardeners.

Alexander Pope wrote, "All gardening is landscape painting." Before you begin your masterpiece, reduce it to paper. Consider such matters as design, climate, sunlight, and, above all, your own tastes.

Thoughtful preparation will pay more dividends than a wheelbarrow full of fertilizer, so remember: Plan your work, then work your plants.

Order is heaven's first law.

Alexander Pope

Plan your work. Without a system, you'll feel swamped.

Norman Vincent Peale

To make a great garden, one must have a great idea or a great opportunity.

Sir George Sitwell

But the noble man makes noble plans, and by noble deeds he stands.

Isaiah 32:8 NIV

As you plan your garden, consider the element of time.
The flowers that bloom in May will not
be blooming in August.

Barbara Damrosch

Plan ahead—it wasn't raining when Noah built the ark.

Anonymous

Although much of the pleasure in gardening derives from
serendipitous effects, thorough planning is essential.

Tom Wright

"I say this because I know what I am planning for you,"
says the Lord. "I have good plans for you, not plans to hurt you.
I will give you hope and a good future."

Jeremiah 29:11 NCV

A place for everything, everything in its place.

Ben Franklin

Well-balanced gardens have a quality of restfulness and exquisite perfection, with plants chosen and placed like words in a perfect poem.

Jeff Cox

It's incredible to realize that what we do each day has meaning in the big picture of God's plan.

Bill Hybels

In his heart a man plans his course,
but the LORD determines his steps.

Proverbs 16:9 NIV

Once you've finalized your plan,
it's time to get your hands dirty.

Burpee Complete Gardener

Nothing takes God by surprise.
Everything is moving according to a plan,
and God wants you in that plan.

Billy Graham

Man masters nature not by force but by understanding.

Jacob Bronowski

There is no wisdom, no insight,
no plan that can succeed against the LORD.

Proverbs 21:30 NIV

Plan your garden on paper.
Mistakes made on paper won't cost you much
in either time or money.

Elsa Bakalar

Too often gardeners start with seed instead of graph paper.

Helen Van Pelt Wilson

Planning a garden on paper is simple—but important.

Jamie Jobb

Unless the LORD builds a house, the work of the builders is useless.

Psalm 127:1 NLT

The wise gardener anticipates June in January.

House and Garden

The one supreme business of life is to find God's plan
for your life and live it.

E. Stanley Jones

No synonym for God is so perfect as Beauty.
Whether as seen carving the lines of the mountains
with glaciers, or gathering matter into stars, or planning
the movements of water, or gardening—still all is Beauty!

John Muir

You will show me the path of life; in Your presence is fullness of joy;
at Your right hand are pleasures forevermore.

Psalm 16:11 NKJV

Your garden plan should leave room for expansion.

Mary Deputy Cassell

The God who created and numbers the stars in the heavens also numbers the hairs of my head. He pays attention to very big things and to very small ones. What matters to me matters to Him, and that changes my life.

Elisabeth Elliot

He who knows what sweets and virtues are in the ground, the waters, the plants, the heavens, and how to come at these enchantments, is the rich and royal man.

Ralph Waldo Emerson

The steps of a good man are ordered by the LORD.

Psalm 37:23 KJV

A Gardener's Prayer

Dear Lord, let my plans be pleasing to You.
Give me the wisdom to plant wisely and
to reap a harvest that honors You and Your Son.
Amen

Beauty

He has made everything beautiful in its time.

Ecclesiastes 3:11 NIV

During World War II, 20 million Americans planted Victory Gardens, and in 1945, after a lengthy competition, a champion Victory Gardener was named. That man was Jim G. Brown, a patriotic Tennessean with a *very* green thumb.

Mr. Brown not only grew the fruits and vegetables that filled his family's table, he also grew the flowers that adorned it. He explained, "Flowers supply our souls with the beauty that is necessary to keep our thoughts in tune with nature."

Are your thoughts in tune with nature? Hopefully so. After all, the noble pursuit of gardening is not only an avocation; it's also a celebration—a celebration of nature's beauty and the One who created it.

Because God created the Natural—invented it out of His love and artistry—it demands our reverence.

C. S. Lewis

God expresses His love through creation.

Charles Stanley

What greater delight is there than to behold the earth appareled with plants as with a robe of embroidered works, set with Orient pearls and garnished with the great diversity of rare and costly jewels. But these delights are in the outward senses. The principle delight is in the mind, singularly enriched with the knowledge of these visible things, setting forth to us the invisible wisdom and admirable workmanship of almighty God.

John Gerard

The heavens declare the glory of God;
and the firmament shows His handiwork.

Psalm 19:1 NKJV

He that sees the beauty of holiness, or true moral good, sees the greatest and most important thing in the world. Unless this is seen, nothing is seen that is worth seeing: for there is no other true excellence or beauty.

Jonathan Edwards

Those who contemplate the beauty of the earth find reserves of strength that will endure.

Rachel Carson

Inasmuch as love grows in you, so beauty grows. For love is the beauty of the soul.

St. Augustine

And let the beauty of the LORD our God be upon us.

Psalm 90:17 KJV

Today you will encounter God's creation.
When you see the beauty around you, let each detail
remind you to lift your head in praise.

Max Lucado

The best remedy for those who are afraid, lonely,
or unhappy is to go outside, somewhere where they can be
quite alone with the heavens, nature, and God.

Anne Frank

If we have a wonderful sense of the divine,
it is because we live amid such awesome magnificence.
If we have refinement of emotion and sensitivity,
it is because of the delicacy, the fragrance,
and indescribable beauty of song and music and
rhythmic movement in the world about us.

Thomas Berry

One thing I have desired of the LORD, that will I seek:
That I may dwell in the house of the LORD all the days of my life,
to behold the beauty of the LORD . . . .

Psalm 27:4 NKJV

If things created are so full of loveliness, how resplendent with beauty must be the One who made them! The wisdom of the Worker is apparent in His handiwork.

Anthony of Padua

No one appreciates the beauty of a majestic shade tree quite like the old man who planted it when he was young.

Marie T. Freeman

Nature is painting for us, day after day, pictures of infinite beauty if only we have the eyes to see them.

John Ruskin

Our Father in heaven, Reveal who you are. Set the world right; Do what's best—as above, so below. Keep us alive with three square meals. Keep us forgiven with you and forgiving others. Keep us safe from ourselves and the Devil. You're in charge! You can do anything you want! You're ablaze in beauty! Yes. Yes. Yes.

Matthew 6:9-13 MSG

God's fingers can touch nothing
but to mould it into loveliness.

George MacDonald

The essence of the beautiful is unity in variety.

Felix Mendelssohn

A man should hear a little music, read a little poetry,
and see a fine picture every day of his life in order
that worldly cares may not obliterate the sense of
the beautiful which God has implanted in the human soul.

Goethe

And the peace of God, which surpasses all understanding,
will guard your hearts and minds through Christ Jesus.
Finally, brethren, whatever things are true, whatever things are noble,
whatever things are just, whatever things are pure, whatever things
are lovely, whatever things are of good report, if there is any virtue
and if there is anything praiseworthy—meditate on these things.

Philippians 4:7-8 NKJV

A Gardener's Prayer

Dear Lord, today I will celebrate Your gifts.
Whether I'm in the garden or not—
whether I'm celebrating a great victory or
enduring an unwelcome disappointment—
I will be a joyful Christian, a worthy example to others,
and a dutiful servant to You.
Amen

Patience

Patience is better than strength.

Proverbs 16:32 NCV

St. Augustine observed, "Patience is the companion of wisdom." Spoken like a true gardener. The plants in our gardens grow at their own pace and will not be hurried by fretful humans. That's why the best gardeners are patient gardeners.

If you're overly anxious for flowers to bloom or seedlings to sprout, slow down and allow God to do His work. God instructs you to be patient in all things—that means being patient with people *and* with gardens. And that's as it should be. After all, think how patient God has been with you.

The principle part of faith is patience.

George MacDonald

A garden is a grand teacher. It teaches patience and careful watchfulness; it teaches industry and thrift; above all it teaches entire trust.

Gertrude Jekyll

Genius is nothing more than a greater aptitude for patience.

Ben Franklin

So don't lose a minute in building on what you've been given, complementing your basic faith with good character, spiritual understanding, alert discipline, passionate patience, reverent wonder, warm friendliness, and generous love, each dimension fitting into and developing the others.

2 Peter 1:5-7 MSG

God never hurries. There are no deadlines against which He must work. To know this is to quiet our spirits and relax our nerves.

A. W. Tozer

Adapt the pace of nature; her secret is patience.

Ralph Waldo Emerson

God gave everyone patience—wise people use it.

Anonymous

Wherefore seeing we also are compassed about with so great a cloud of witnesses, let us lay aside every weight, and the sin which doth so easily beset us, and let us run with patience the race that is set before us . . . .

Hebrews 12:1 KJV

It is wise to wait because God gives clear direction only when we are willing to wait.

Charles Stanley

A man watches his pear tree day after day, impatient for the ripening of the fruit. Let him attempt to force the ripening fruit, and he may spoil both fruit and tree. But, let him patiently wait, and the ripe pear, at length, falls into his lap.

Abraham Lincoln

We must never think that patience is complacency. Patience is endurance in action.

Warren Wiersbe

Yet the LORD longs to be gracious to you; he rises to show you compassion. For the LORD is a God of justice. Blessed are all who wait for him!

Isaiah 30:18 NIV

Grass that is here today and gone tomorrow does not require much time to mature. A big oak tree that lasts for generations requires much more time to grow and mature. God is concerned about your life through eternity. Allow Him to take all the time He needs to shape you for His purposes. Larger assignments will require longer periods of preparation.

Henry Blackaby

Patient waiting is often the highest way of doing God's will.

St. Francis de Sales

Our patience will achieve more than our force.

Edmund Burke

My brethren, count it all joy when you fall into various trials, knowing that the testing of your faith produces patience. But let patience have its perfect work, that you may be perfect and complete, lacking nothing.

James 1:2-4 NKJV

Waiting is the hardest kind of work, but God knows best, and we may joyfully leave all in His hands.

Lottie Moon

In all negotiations of difficulties, a man may not look to sow and reap at once; but must prepare business and so ripen it by degrees.

Francis Bacon

Who longest waits most surely wins.

Helen Hunt Jackson

Patience is better than pride.

Ecclesiastes 7:8 NLT

God is never in a hurry.

Oswald Chambers

Sometimes in life the best and hardest thing to do is nothing.

J. R. Freeman

There is no great achievement that is not the result of patient working and waiting.

Josiah Gilbert Holland

Enthusiasm without knowledge is not good. If you act too quickly, you might make a mistake.

Proverbs 19:2 NCV

Never be in a hurry; do everything quietly and in a calm spirit. Do not lose your inner peace for anything whatsoever, even if your whole world seems upset.

St. Francis de Sales

Teach us, O Lord, the disciplines of patience, for to wait is often harder than to work.

Peter Marshall

All things pass. Patience attains all it strives for.

St. Teresa of Avila

Be still before the LORD and wait patiently for Him.

Psalm 37:7 NIV

A Gardener's Prayer

Dear Lord, give me the wisdom to be patient.
When I'm in a hurry for the flowers to bloom,
give me peace. When I am frustrated by
the inevitable ups and downs of life,
give me perspective. When I am angry,
keep me mindful of Your presence.
Let me trust Your plans, Lord—with patience
and thanksgiving—today and always.
Amen

Diligence

Now the one who plants and the one who waters are equal,
and each will receive his own reward according to his own labor.

1 Corinthians 3:8 HCSB

A garden, like so many other things in life, rewards diligence. More often than not, the soil is a fair judge of one's work: the size of one's harvest tends to be proportional to the size of one's efforts.

Thankfully, the work of gardening isn't really work in the strictest sense. The experience of digging in the moist earth is one of nature's sublime pleasures. But make no mistake: in the garden, sublime pleasure and hard work go hand-in-hand.

Gardening may be a labor of love, but it is still labor. The self-tending garden has yet to be invented—hopefully, it never will be. After all, what would a garden be without the work of gardening? A grocery store.

Great relief and satisfaction can come from seeking
God's priorities for us in each season, discerning what is
"best" in the midst of many noble opportunities,
and pouring our most excellent energies into those things.

Beth Moore

Those who labor in the earth are the chosen people of God.

Thomas Jefferson

I long to accomplish a great and noble task,
but it is my chief duty to accomplish small tasks
as if they were great and noble.

Helen Keller

Do all you can to live a peaceful life. Take care of your own business,
and do your own work as we have already told you. If you do,
then people who are not believers will respect you,
and you will not have to depend on others for what you need.

1 Thessalonians 4:11-12 NCV

We are expected to use all available means.
We are not allowed to be idle and do nothing simply
because we say we are trusting in providence.

C. H. Spurgeon

Plough deep while sluggards sleep;
and you shall have corn to sell and to keep.

Ben Franklin

Christians are to "labor," which refers to hard, manual work.
Hard work is honorable. As Christians we should work hard
so that we will have enough to give to those in need,
not so that we will have more of what we don't need.

John MacArthur

But if anyone does not provide for his own, and especially
for those of his household, he has denied the faith and
is worse than an unbeliever.

1 Timothy 5:8 NASB

Thank God every morning when you get up that you have something which must be done, whether you like it or not. Work breeds a hundred virtues that idleness never knows.

Charles Kingsley

On Saturday evening, when we listen to the radio and shell our dried beans, we are able to relax after our week's work and realize that there is more happiness in simple living than in glamour.

Jim G. Brown

Hoping for a good future without investing in today is like a farmer waiting for a crop without ever planting any seed.

John Maxwell

He did it with all his heart. So he prospered.

2 Chronicles 31:21 NKJV

Work is doing it. Discipline is doing it every day.
Diligence is doing it well every day.

Dave Ramsey

Pray for a good harvest, but continue to hoe.

Anonymous

The world does not consider labor a blessing, therefore it flees and hates it, but the pious who fear the Lord labor with a ready and cheerful heart, for they know God's command, and they acknowledge His calling.

Martin Luther

But this I say: He who sows sparingly will also reap sparingly, and he who sows bountifully will also reap bountifully.

2 Corinthians 9:6 NKJV

It may be that the day of judgment will dawn tomorrow; in that case, we shall gladly stop working for a better tomorrow. But not before.

Dietrich Bonhoeffer

The first rule of successful gardening is to work with, not against, the natural setting.

Burpee Complete Gardener

Think enthusiastically about everything, especially your work.

Norman Vincent Peale

Even while we were with you, we gave you this rule: "Whoever does not work should not eat."

2 Thessalonians 3:10 NLT

All work, if offered to Him, is transformed.
It is not secular but sacred, sanctified in the glad offering.

Elisabeth Elliot

We are thankful to Thee for sunshine and rain and
also for health and strength to enable us to work
with Nature "from dawn to the setting sun."

Jim G. Brown's Thanksgiving Prayer for 1945

Dear Lord, let us pray for our daily bread,
but let us not be afraid to hunt for our corn-pone
with sweat running down the hoe handle.

Sam Jones

Work hard so God can approve you. Be a good worker,
one who does not need to be ashamed and
who correctly explains the word of truth.

2 Timothy 2:15 NLT

I seem to have been led, little by little, toward my work; and I believe that the same fact will appear in the life of anyone who will cultivate such powers as God has given him and then go on, bravely, quietly, but persistently, doing such work as comes to his hands.

Fanny Crosby

Show me your garden and I shall tell you what you are.

Alfred Austin

Let us work as if success depends on us alone, but with the heartfelt conviction that we are doing nothing and God everything.

St. Ignatius Loyola

Whatever you do, do your work heartily, as for the Lord rather than for men.

Colossians 3:23 NASB

A Gardener's Prayer

Lord, I know that You desire a bountiful harvest for all Your children. But, You have instructed us that we must sow before we reap, not after. Help me, Lord, to sow the seeds of Your abundance everywhere I go. Let me be diligent in all my undertakings and give me patience to wait for Your harvest. In time, Lord, let me reap the harvest that is found in Your will for my life. Amen

The Optimistic Gardener

Let us hold on to the confession of our hope without wavering, for He who promised is faithful.

Hebrews 10:23 HCSB

Gardeners are, by nature, an optimistic lot. They gladly sink money, effort and time into a plot of ground with no guarantee of return. Planting a garden is truly faith in action.

In this chapter, we consider one of the gardener's most useful tools: a highly cultivated sense of optimism. Why is an upbeat attitude so essential? Because in the garden, there are too many other things to worry about without adding the self-fulfilling prophecy to the list.

If you're a gardener—or if you're not—sow seeds of optimism. They're guaranteed to sprout.

The people whom I have seen succeed best in life have always been cheerful and hopeful people who went about their business with a smile on their faces.

Charles Kingsley

A garden is never so good as it will be next year.

Thomas Cooper

Never yield to gloomy anticipation.
Place your hope and confidence in God.
He has no record of failure.

Mrs. Charles E. Cowman

Now faith is the substance of things hoped for, the evidence of things not seen.

Hebrews 11:1 KJV

Faith not only can help you through a crisis,
it can help you to approach life after the hard times
with a whole new perspective. It can help you adopt
an outlook of hope and courage through faith to face reality.

John Maxwell

In God's wildness lies the hope of the world—
the great fresh unblighted, unredeemed wilderness.
The galling harness of civilization drops off,
and the wounds heal ere we are aware.

John Muir

Keep your feet on the ground, but let your heart soar
as high as it will. Refuse to be average or to surrender
to the chill of your spiritual environment.

A. W. Tozer

Full of hope, you'll relax, confident again;
you'll look around, sit back, and take it easy.

Job 11:18 MSG

I wish I could make it all new again; I can't. But God can. "He restores my soul," wrote the shepherd. God doesn't reform; he restores. He doesn't camouflage the old; he restores the new. The Master Builder will pull out the original plan and restore it. He will restore the vigor; he will restore the energy. He will restore the hope. He will restore the soul.

Max Lucado

He who plants a tree, plants a hope.

Anonymous

The essence of optimism is that it takes no account of the present, but it is a source of inspiration, of vitality, and of hope. Where others have resigned, it enables a man to hold his head high, to claim the future for himself, and not abandon it to his enemy.

Dietrich Bonhoeffer

Happy is he . . .whose hope is in the LORD his God.

Psalm 146:5 KJV

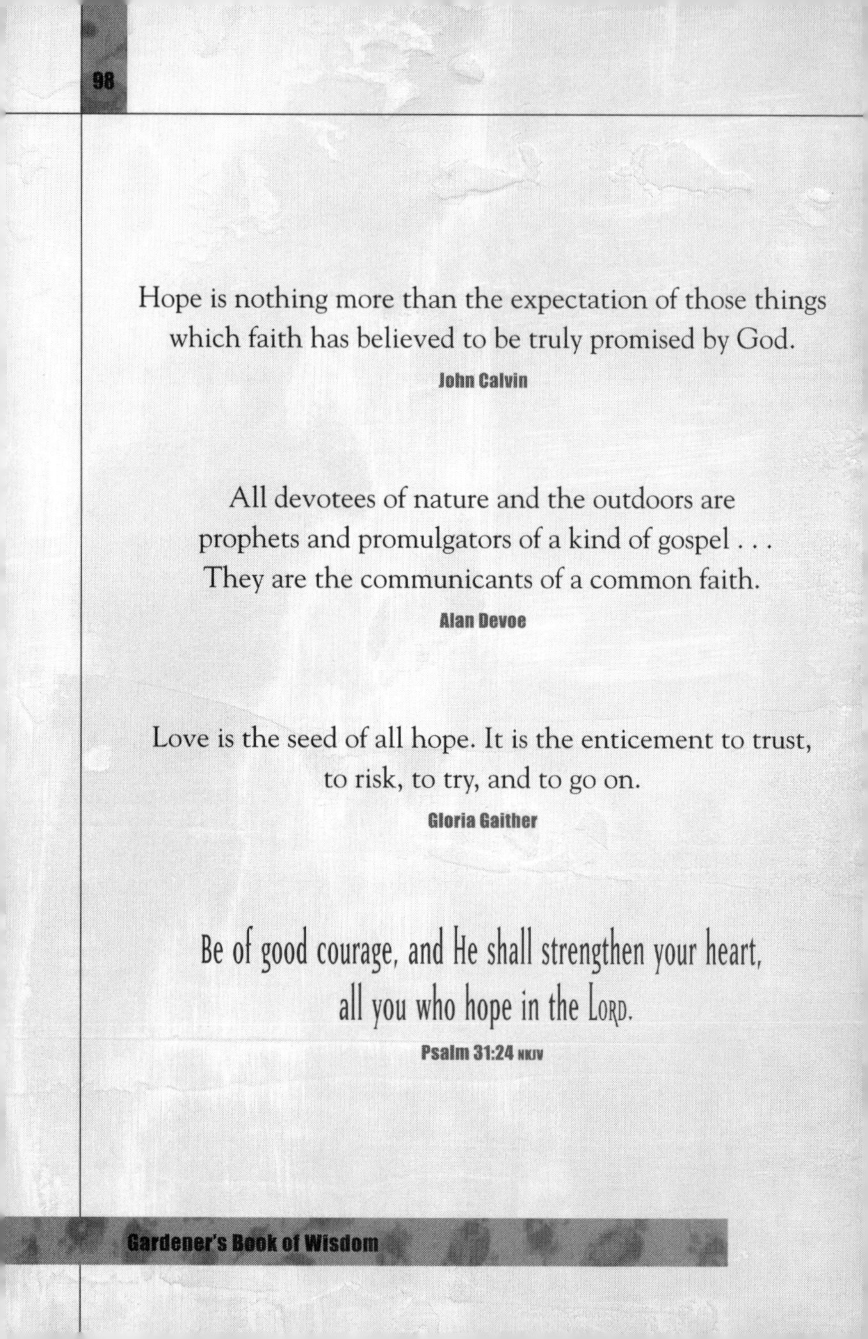

Hope is nothing more than the expectation of those things which faith has believed to be truly promised by God.

John Calvin

All devotees of nature and the outdoors are prophets and promulgators of a kind of gospel . . . They are the communicants of a common faith.

Alan Devoe

Love is the seed of all hope. It is the enticement to trust, to risk, to try, and to go on.

Gloria Gaither

Be of good courage, and He shall strengthen your heart, all you who hope in the LORD.

Psalm 31:24 NKJV

Great hopes make great men.

Thomas Fuller

I believe that the Creator of this universe takes delight in turning the terrors and tragedies that come with living in this old, fallen domain of the devil and transforming them into something that strengthens our hope, tests our faith, and shows forth His glory.

Al Green

Faith looks back and draws courage; hope looks ahead and keeps desire alive.

John Eldredge

I find rest in God; only he gives me hope.

Psalm 62:5 NCV

To own a bit of ground, to scratch it with a hoe,
to plant seeds, and watch the renewal of life—
this is the commonest delight of the race,
the most satisfactory thing a man can do.

Charles Dudley Warner

God is the only one who can make
the valley of trouble a door of hope.

Catherine Marshall

The best we can hope for in this life is a knothole peek
at the shining realities ahead. Yet a glimpse is enough.
It's enough to convince our hearts that whatever sufferings
and sorrows currently assail us aren't worthy of
comparison to that which waits over the horizon.

Joni Eareckson Tada

May the God of hope fill you with all joy and peace
as you trust in him, so that you may overflow with hope
by the power of the Holy Spirit.

Romans 15:13 NIV

All through the long winter, I dream of my garden.
On the first day of spring, I dig my fingers deep into
the soft earth. I can feel its energy, and my spirits soar.

Helen Hayes

When you accept the fact that sometimes seasons are
dry and times are hard and that God is in control of both,
you will discover a sense of divine refuge because
the hope then is in God and not in yourself.

Charles Swindoll

Everything that is done in the world is done by hope.

Martin Luther

But if we hope for what we do not yet have, we wait for it patiently.

Romans 8:25 NIV

If seeds in the black earth can turn into such beautiful roses,
what might not the heart of man become
in its long journey toward the stars?

G. K. Chesterton

The hope we have in Jesus is the anchor for
the soul—something sure and steadfast, preventing drifting
or giving way, lowered to the depth of God's love.

Franklin Graham

Christ has turned all our sunsets into dawn.

St. Clement of Alexandria

Make me hear joy and gladness.

Psalm 51:8 NKJV

Nature's door is always open, her treasures, and often her terrors, on display. Nature unfailingly responds to our overtures in surprising and unexpected ways that can comfort, startle, amuse, charm, and challenge us.

F. Lynne Bachleda

All things are possible for him who believes, more to him who hopes, even more to him who loves.

St. Lawrence of Brindisi

Dark as my path may seem to others, I carry a magic light in my heart. Faith, the spiritual strong searchlight, illumines the way, and although sinister doubts lurk in the shadow, I walk unafraid toward the enchanted wood where the foliage is always green, where joy abides, where nightingales nest and sing, and where life and death are one in the presence of the Lord.

Helen Keller

I can do everything through him that gives me strength.

Philippians 4:13 NIV

A Gardener's Prayer

Lord, help me be an optimist whether I'm in my garden or not. Let me expect the best from You, and let me look for the best in others. Let me trust You, Lord, to direct every aspect of my life. And, let me be Your faithful, hopeful, optimistic servant every day that I live.
Amen

Time

So teach us to number our days,
that we may gain a heart of wisdom.

Psalm 90:12 NKJV

The third chapter of Ecclesiastes reminds us that, "To every thing there is a season, and a time to every purpose under the heaven" (3:1 KJV). These words apply to all of life's endeavors, including gardening. In the garden, each passing season has its own special beauty and its own special purpose.

The message of every garden is the same: Sow, reap, and share—while there is still time.

Every day, like every life, is composed of moments. Each moment of your life holds within it the potential to seek God's will and to serve His purposes. If you are wise, you will strive to do both.

How will you invest the time that God has given you? Will you savor the moments of your life, or will you squander them? Will you use your time as an instrument of God's will, or will you allow commonplace distractions to rule your day and your life?

The gift of time is a gift from God. Treat it as if it were a precious, fleeting, one-of-a-kind treasure. Because it is.

To know and be known by Nature requires nothing more
and nothing less than spending time with her
as we would a cherished friend—listening,
looking, revealing, laughing, crying, and praying together.

F. Lynne Bachleda

Flowers may beckon us, but they speak
toward heaven and God.

Henry Ward Beecher

Our time is short! The time we can invest for God,
in creative things, in receiving our fellowmen for Christ,
is short!

Billy Graham

Lord, tell me when the end will come and how long I will live.
Let me know how long I have. You have given me only a short life;
my lifetime is like nothing to you. Everyone's life is only a breath.

Psalm 39:4-5 NCV

Does God care about all the responsibilities we have to juggle in our daily lives? Of course. But he cares more that our lives demonstrate balance, the ability to discern what is essential and give ourselves fully to it.

Penelope Stokes

To every thing there is a season, and a time to every purpose under the heaven: A time to be born, and a time to die; a time to plant, and a time to pluck up that which is planted; A time to kill, and a time to heal; a time to break down, and a time to build up; A time to weep, and a time to laugh; a time to mourn, and a time to dance; A time to cast away stones, and a time to gather stones together; a time to embrace, and a time to refrain from embracing; A time to get, and a time to lose; a time to keep, and a time to cast away; A time to rend, and a time to sew; a time to keep silence, and a time to speak; A time to love, and a time to hate; a time of war, and a time of peace.

Ecclesiastes 3:1-8 KJV

It is a commonplace of all religious thought,
even the most primitive, that the man seeking visions and
insight must go apart from his fellows and
live for a time in the wilderness.

Loren Eiseley

Life's unfolding stops for no one.

Kathy Troccoli

I've finally realized that if something has
no significant value, it doesn't deserve my time.
Life is not a dress rehearsal, and I'll never get this day again.

Sheri Rose Shepherd

Let us not become weary in doing good,
for at the proper time we will reap a harvest
if we do not give up.

Galatians 6:9 NIV

Nature gives to every time and season some beauties of its own; and from morning to night, as from the cradle to the grave, is but a succession of changes so gentle and easy that we can scarcely mark their progress.

Charles Dickens

The more time you give to something,
the more you reveal its importance and value to you.

Rick Warren

Time is what we want most, but what, alas, we use worst, and for which God will surely most strictly reckon with us when time shall be no more.

William Penn

I will bless them and the places surrounding my hill.
I will send down showers in season;
there will be showers of blessings.

Ezekiel 34:26 NIV

God has a present will for your life. It is neither chaotic nor utterly exhausting. In the midst of many good choices vying for your time, He will give you the discernment to recognize what is best.

Beth Moore

I hate to be reminded of the passage of time, and in a garden of flowers one can never escape from it.

E. V. Lucas

Time cannot be recycled.

Anonymous

But when the fullness of the time had come, God sent forth His Son, born of a woman, born under the law, to redeem those who were under the law, that we might receive the adoption as sons.

Galatians 4:4-5 NKJV

No winter lasts forever, no spring skips its turn.
April is a promise that May is bound to keep,
and we know it.

Hal Borland

Our leisure, even our play, is a matter of serious concern.
There is no neutral ground in the universe:
every square inch, every split second,
is claimed by God and counterclaimed by Satan.

C. S. Lewis

Time isn't a commodity, something you pass around
like cake. Time is the substance of life.
When anyone asks you to give your time,
they're really asking for a chunk of your life.

Antoinette Bosco

Timely advice is as lovely as golden apples in a silver basket.

Proverbs 25:11 NLT

Things seem to move very slowly in a garden.
But nothing ever remains the same.

Jamie Jobb

Frustration is not the will of God.
There is time to do anything and everything
that God wants us to do.

Elisabeth Elliot

May you live all the days of your life.

Jonathan Swift

Give your entire attention to what God is doing right now, and don't get worked up about what may or may not happen tomorrow. God will help you deal with whatever hard things come up when the time comes.

Matthew 6:34 MSG

A Gardener's Prayer

Dear Lord, You have given me a wonderful gift:
time here on earth. Let me use it wisely—
for the glory of Your kingdom and
the betterment of Your world.
Amen

God's Presence

Fear not, for I am with you; Be not dismayed,
for I am your God. I will strengthen you.

Isaiah 41:10 NKJV

In the garden, we sense God's presence and His love. And as God's children, we are called to return the Father's love.

Christ made it clear: our first and greatest commandment is that we love God with all our hearts. When we worship God with faith and assurance, when we place Him at the absolute center of our lives, we invite His love into our hearts. When we do so, we are blessed beyond measure and beyond words.

St. Augustine wrote, "I love you, Lord, not doubtingly, but with absolute certainty. Your Word beat upon my heart until I fell in love with you, and now the universe and everything in it tells me to love you." Let us pray that we, too, will turn our hearts to our Father and to His Son. When we do, we are blessed in this life and throughout all eternity.

We have no time to sin when we devote our time
to working in the garden with God.

Jim G. Brown

We should learn to live in the presence of the living God.
He should be a well for us: delightful, comforting, unfailing,
springing up to eternal life (John 4:14). When we rely on
other people, their water supplies ultimately dry up.
But, the well of the Creator never fails to nourish us.

C. H. Spurgeon

God is making the world, and the show is so grand and
beautiful and exciting that I have never been
able to study any other.

John Muir

Draw near to God, and He will draw near to you.

James 4:8 HCSB

All are but parts of one stupendous whole,
Whose body nature is, and God the soul.

Alexander Pope

Where is God? He's right here at your side, my friend.
He never left.

Charles Swindoll

When I first open my eyes upon the morning meadows and
look out upon the beautiful world,
I thank God I am alive.

Ralph Waldo Emerson

Be strong and courageous! Do not tremble or be dismayed,
for the LORD your God is with you wherever you go.

Joshua 1:9 NASB

Nature . . . is God's daughter.

Francis Thompson

God walks with us. He scoops us up in His arms or simply sits with us in silent strength until we cannot avoid the awesome recognition that yes, even now, He is here.

Gloria Gaither

The hills are mute, but how they speak of God!

Charles Hansom Towne

The eyes of the LORD are in every place, keeping watch . . . .

Proverbs 15:3 NKJV

Nature is an unlimited broadcasting station through which God speaks to us every hour—if we will only tune in.

George Washington Carver

A sense of deity is inscribed on every heart.

John Calvin

Earth's crammed with heaven,
And every common bush afire with God.

Elizabeth Barrett Browning

Where can I go from your Spirit? Where can I flee from your presence? If I go up to the heavens, you are there; if I make my bed in the depths, you are there. If I rise on the wings of the dawn, if I settle on the far side of the sea, even there your hand will guide me, your right hand will hold me fast.

Psalm 139:7-10 NIV

Nature is the living, visible garment of God.

Goethe

It's a crazy world and life speeds by at a blur, yet God is right in the middle of the craziness. And anywhere, at anytime, we may turn to Him, hear His voice, feel His hand, and catch the fragrance of heaven.

Joni Eareckson Tada

Man must feel the earth to know himself and recognize his values . . . God made life simple. It is man who complicates it.

Charles A. Lindbergh

You will show me the way of life, granting me the joy of your presence and the pleasures of living with you forever.

Psalm 16:11 NLT

Nature is full of genius, full of the divinity;
so that not a snowflake escapes its fashioning hand.

Henry David Thoreau

Help us to make at once the amendments in our lives that are necessary before we can experience the true meaning of the words "in thy presence is fullness of joy."

A. W. Tozer

It's been said that when God sends you on a journey, He will direct your path and light your way, even if it's only one step at a time. And from walking the mountains and valleys of my own life, I believe that to be true. When the Lord is with me, I can feel his presence and move out in confidence, and although I may not know my final destination, I have his assurance that I'm heading in the right direction.

Al Green

For the eyes of the Lord range throughout the earth to strengthen those whose hearts are fully committed to him.

2 Chronicles 16:9 NIV

Look through nature up to nature's God.

Alexander Pope

Get yourself into the presence of the loving Father.
Just place yourself before Him, and look up into His face;
think of His love, His wonderful, tender, pitying love.

Andrew Murray

I know that for the right practice, in the presence of God,
the heart must be empty of all other things, because God
will possess the heart alone; and as he cannot possess it
alone without emptying it of all besides,
so neither can He act there, and do in it what He pleases,
unless it be left vacant to Him.

Brother Lawrence

Let your character be free from the love of money,
being content with what you have; for He Himself has said,
"I will never desert you, nor will I ever forsake you."

Hebrews 13:5 NASB

A Gardener's Prayer

Dear Lord, You are with me always.
Help me feel Your presence in every situation and every circumstance. Today, Dear God, let me feel You and acknowledge Your presence, Your love, and Your Son.
Amen

Wisdom

So teach us to number our days, that we may gain a heart of wisdom.

Psalm 90:12 NKJV

Tending a garden helps you maintain perspective. When the events of life seem out of balance, your garden is the perfect place to vanquish the stresses and strains of everyday living. And, of course, your garden is a wonderful place to remind yourself of God's timeless truths.

Today, as you survey that little patch of ground that God has entrusted to your care, take time to ponder the wisdom of God's unchanging Word. The wisdom of the world changes with the ever-shifting sands of public opinion. God's wisdom does not. His wisdom is eternal. It never changes. And it most certainly is the wisdom that you must use to plan your day, your life, and your eternal destiny.

I need the spiritual revival that comes from spending quiet time alone with Jesus in prayer and in thoughtful meditation on His Word.

Anne Graham Lotz

Cultivate the garden within.

Anonymous

Wise people listen to wise instruction, especially instruction from the Word of God.

Warren Wiersbe

The godly give good advice, but fools are destroyed by their lack of common sense.

Proverbs 10:21 NLT

Never, no never, did Nature say one thing,
and wisdom another.

Edmond Burke

If you lack knowledge, go to school.
If you lack wisdom, get on your knees.

Vance Havner

The wilderness holds answers to questions
man has not yet learned to ask.

Nancy Newhall

The Lord says, "I will make you wise and show you where to go.
I will guide you and watch over you."

Psalm 32:8 NCV

True wisdom consists in not departing from nature and in molding our conduct to her laws and models.

Seneca

Patience is the companion of wisdom.

St. Augustine

Give me a spark of Nature's fire.
That's all the learning I desire.

Robert Burns

The fear of the LORD is the beginning of wisdom; a good understanding have all those who do His commandments. His praise endures forever.

Psalm 111:10 NKJV

He who has known how to love the land has loved eternity.

Stefan Zeromski

Knowledge can be learned, but wisdom must be earned.
Wisdom is knowledge . . . lived.

Sheila Walsh

You will find something more in woods than in books.
Trees and stones will teach that
which you can never learn from masters.

Saint Bernard

Choose my instruction instead of silver, knowledge rather than
choice gold, for wisdom is more precious than rubies,
and nothing you desire can compare with her.

Proverbs 8:10-11 NIV

The more wisdom enters our hearts,
the more we will be able to trust our hearts
in difficult situations.

John Eldredge

As parents, we can take our children with us to the land.
We can be there with them as they climb on rocks,
play in streams and waves, dig in the rich soil of woods and
gardens, putter and learn. Here, on the land,
we learn from each other.
Here, our children's journey begins.

Stephen Trimble

Wisdom is a tree of life to those who embrace her;
happy are those who hold her tightly.

Proverbs 3:18 NLT

A flower is an educated weed.

Luther Burbank

A prudent question is one-half of wisdom.

Francis Bacon

The river has taught me to listen; you will learn from it, too. The river knows everything; one can learn everything from it. You have already learned from the river that it is good to strive downwards, to sink, to seek the depths.

Herman Hesse

Make your ear attentive to wisdom,
incline your heart to understanding.

Proverbs 2:2 NASB

Wisdom is the God-given ability to see life with rare objectivity and to handle life with rare stability.

Charles Swindoll

A gardener learns more in the mistakes than in the successes.

Barbara Dodge Borland

Wisdom takes us beyond the realm of mere right and wrong. Wisdom takes into account our personalities, our strengths, our weaknesses, and even our present state of mind.

Charles Stanley

But the wisdom that is from above is first pure, then peaceable, gentle, willing to yield, full of mercy and good fruits, without partiality and without hypocrisy.

James 3:17 NKJV

A Gardener's Prayer

Dear Lord, when I trust in the wisdom of the world,
I am often led astray, but when I trust in Your wisdom,
I build my life upon a firm foundation.
Today and every day I will trust Your Word and
follow it, knowing that the ultimate wisdom is
Your wisdom and the ultimate truth is Your truth.
Amen

The Harvest

Then he said to his disciples,
"The harvest is plentiful but the workers are few.
Ask the Lord of the harvest, therefore, to send out workers
into his harvest field."

Matthew 9:37 NIV

If you're a disciplined gardener, then you know that the job of tending your little patch of ground requires work and plenty of it. But God is not complaining, and neither should you.

God's Holy Word is clear: He expects His children to do the work *first* and reap the harvest *second.* So, whether you're in the garden or outside it, your success will depend, in large part, upon the quality and quantity of your work.

Our Heavenly Father has created a world in which hard work is honored and idleness is not. We reside in that world, so we should live—and we should garden—accordingly.

I am more and more persuaded that all that is
required of us is faithful seed-sowing.
The harvest is bound to follow.

Annie Armstrong

The evangelistic harvest is always urgent.
The destiny of men and of nations is always being decided.
Every generation is strategic. We are not responsible for
the past generation, and we cannot bear the full
responsibility for the next one, but we do have
our generation. God will hold us responsible as to
how well we fulfill our responsibilities to this age and
take advantage of our opportunities.

Billy Graham

Go to the ant, you slacker! Observe its ways and become wise.
Without leader, administrator, or ruler, it prepares its provisions
in summer; it gathers its food during harvest. How long will you stay
in bed, you slacker? When will you get up from your sleep?

Proverbs 6:6-9 HCSB

Who loves a garden still his Eden keeps,
perennial pleasures plants and wholesome harvest reaps.

Bronson Alcott

Here, then, is the secret of endurance when the going is tough: God is producing a harvest in our lives. He wants the "fruit of the Spirit" to grow (Galatians 5:22-23), and the only way He can do it is through trials and troubles.

Warren Wiersbe

Let every Christian be a gardener so that he and she and the whole creation which groans in expectation of the Spirit's final harvest may inherit paradise.

Vigen Guroian

No discipline seems pleasant at the time, but painful. Later on, however, it produces a harvest of righteousness and peace for those who have been trained by it.

Hebrews 12:11 NIV

Your life is not a boring stretch of highway.
It's a straight line to heaven. And just look at the fields ripening along the way. Look at the tenacity and endurance.
Look at the grains of righteousness.
You'll have quite a crop at harvest . . . so don't give up!

Joni Eareckson Tada

To have the harvest we must sow the seed.

Liberty Hyde Bailey

We are now, a very, very few feeble workers, scattering the grain broadcast according as time and strength permit. God will give the harvest; doubt it not.
But the laborers are few.

Lottie Moon

Let us not become weary in doing good, for at the proper time we will reap a harvest if we do not give up.

Galatians 6:9 NIV

God has promised that if we harvest well
with the tools of thanksgiving,
there will be seeds for planting in the spring.

Gloria Gaither

At harvest time, the vegetable garden comes into
the kitchen. Not all at once, unfortunately.

Barbara Dodge Borland

All of humanity is engaged in worship. The question is not
whether human beings worship, but what they worship.
Wise men and women choose to worship God.
When they do, they are blessed with a plentiful harvest of
joy, peace, and abundance.

Marie T. Freeman

I am the Vine, you are the branches.
When you're joined with me and I with you, the relation intimate and
organic, the harvest is sure to be abundant.

John 15:5 MSG

Don't judge each day by the harvest you reap,
but by the seeds you plant.

Robert Louis Stevenson

The two keys to success in gardening are understanding how plants grow and understanding how to provide them with a better home.

Sheryl London

Each part of life has its own abundant harvest, to be garnered in season. Old age is rich in blessings.

Cicero

For seven days celebrate the Feast to the LORD your God at the place the LORD will choose. For the LORD your God will bless you in all your harvest and in all the work of your hands, and your joy will be complete.

Deuteronomy 16:15 NIV

The law of harvest is to reap more than you sow. Sow an act, and you reap a habit. Sow a habit and you reap a character. Sow a character and you reap a destiny.

James Allen

The seeds of failure, when they are properly sown and carefully tended, can yield a bountiful harvest of success.

Jim Gallery

After these things the Lord appointed other seventy also, and sent them two and two before his face into every city and place, whither he himself would come. Therefore said he unto them, The harvest truly is great, but the laborers are few: pray ye therefore the Lord of the harvest, that he would send forth laborers into his harvest. Go your ways: behold, I send you forth as lambs among wolves.

Luke 10:1-3 KJV

Having harvested all the knowledge and wisdom
we can from our mistakes and failures,
we should put them behind us and go ahead.

Edith Johnson

Study nature as the countenance of God.

Charles Kingsley

It is only the farmer who faithfully plants seeds
in the spring who reaps a harvest in August.

B. C. Forbes

Those who wait for perfect weather will never plant seeds;
those who look at every cloud will never harvest crops.
Plant early in the morning, and work until evening, because
you don't know if this or that will succeed. They might both do well.

Ecclesiastes 11:4, 6 NCV

A Gardener's Prayer

Dear Lord, You have given me another day of life.
Today, let me be successful in Your eyes.
Help me, Father, see more clearly the path You have
chosen for me. Enable me to sow, to reap,
and to give thanks for Your creation,
for Your love, and for Your Son.
Amen

Thanksgiving

Come, let us sing to the Lord! Let us give a joyous shout to the rock of our salvation! Let us come before him with thanksgiving. Let us sing him psalms of praise.

Psalm 95:1-2 NLT

Dietrich Bonhoeffer observed, "It is only with gratitude that life becomes rich." These words certainly apply to every gardener, including you.

Are you a grateful gardener? Do you appreciate the gifts that God has given you? And, do you demonstrate your gratitude by being a faithful steward of the gifts and talents that you have received from your Creator? You most certainly should be thankful. After all, when you stop to think about it, God has given you more blessings than you can count. So the question of the day is this: will you thank your Heavenly Father . . . or will you spend your time and energy doing other things?

God is always listening—are you willing to say thanks? It's up to you, and the next move is yours.

Thanksgiving invites God to bestow a second benefit.

Robert Herrick

Gratitude to God makes even a temporal blessing a taste of heaven.

William Romaine

The words "thank" and "think" come from the same root word. If we would think more, we would thank more.

Warren Wiersbe

And let the peace of God rule in your hearts, to which also you were called in one body; and be thankful.

Colossians 3:15 NKJV

We should spend as much time in thanking God
for his benefits as we do asking him for them.

St. Vincent de Paul

No duty is more urgent than that of returning thanks.

St. Ambrose

Thank God every morning when you get up that you
have something to do that day which must be done,
whether you like it or not.

Charles Kingsley

Thanks be to God for His indescribable gift!

2 Corinthians 9:15 NKJV

Weather means more when you have a garden. There's nothing like listening to a shower and thinking how it is soaking in and around your lettuce and green beans.

Marcelene Cox

God is worthy of our praise and is pleased when we come before Him with thanksgiving.

Shirley Dobson

The best way to show my gratitude to God is to accept everything, even my problems, with joy.

Mother Teresa

Give thanks in all circumstances; for this is God's will for you in Christ Jesus.

1 Thessalonians 5:18 NIV

The act of thanksgiving is a demonstration of the fact that you are going to trust and believe God.

Kay Arthur

Thanksgiving is good but Thanksliving is better.

Jim Gallery

Anywhere you live you can find room for a garden somewhere.

Jamie Jobb

Make a joyful noise unto the LORD all ye lands. Serve the LORD with gladness: come before his presence with singing. Know ye that the LORD he is God: it is he that hath made us, and not we ourselves; we are his people and the sheep of his pasture. Enter into his gates with thanksgiving, and into his courts with praise; be thankful unto him and bless his name. For the LORD is good; his mercy is everlasting; and his truth endureth to all generations.

Psalm 100 KJV

All gardens are a form of autobiography.

Robert Dash

Thanksgiving or complaining—these words express two contrastive attitudes of the souls of God's children in regard to His dealings with them. The soul that gives thanks can find comfort in everything; the soul that complains can find comfort in nothing.

Hannah Whitall Smith

When it comes to life, the critical thing is whether you take things for granted or take them with gratitude.

G. K. Chesterton

If I eat what is served to me, grateful to God for what is on the table, how can I worry about what someone will say? I thanked God for it and he blessed it!

1 Corinthians 10:30 MSG

God has promised that if we harvest well
with the tools of thanksgiving,
there will be seeds for planting in the spring.

Gloria Gaither

A Christian who walks by faith accepts all circumstances
from God. He thanks God when everything goes good,
when everything goes bad,
and for the "blues" somewhere in between.
He thanks God whether he feels like it or not.

Erwin Lutzer

Seeds of discouragement will not grow in a thankful heart.

Anonymous

Praise the LORD! Oh give thanks to the LORD,
for He is good; For His lovingkindness is everlasting.

Psalm 106:1 NASB

It is always possible to be thankful for what is given rather than to complain about what is not given.
One or the other becomes a habit of life.

Elisabeth Elliot

Gardening is medicine that does not need a prescription.

Anonymous

The game was to just find something about everything to be glad about—no matter what it was.
You see, when you're hunting for the glad things, you sort of forget the other kind.

Eleanor H. Porter

You are my God, and I will give you thanks; you are my God, and I will exalt you. Give thanks to the LORD, for he is good; his love endures forever.

Psalm 118:28-29 NIV

I think the true gardener, the older he grows,
should more and more develop a humble, grateful spirit.

Reginald Farrer

It is only with gratitude that life becomes rich.

Dietrich Bonhoeffer

We ought to give thanks for all fortune: if it is good,
because it is good, if bad, because it works in us patience,
humility, and the contempt of this world along
with the hope of our eternal country.

C. S. Lewis

All Your works shall give thanks to You, O LORD,
And Your godly ones shall bless You.

Psalm 145:10 NASB

A child of God should be a visible beatitude for joy
and a living doxology for gratitude.

C. H. Spurgeon

Be careful. If you let yourself feel this wonder,
you will be lost. You will never get over it.
The consequences will be dramatic, and you risk being
labeled an eccentric by your fellow humans: life will begin
to make sense; meaning will come into your life unbidden;
doubt will drop away and you will know who you are.

James Thornton

We give strength to our souls as we train ourselves to speak
words of thankfulness and praise.

Annie Chapman

I will give thanks to the LORD with all my heart;
I will tell of all Your wonders. I will be glad and exult in You;
I will sing praise to Your name, O Most High.

Psalm 9:1-2 NASB

A Gardener's Prayer

Dear Lord, You have given me a plentiful harvest, and You want to give me even more. But sometimes, amid the demands of the day, I lose perspective, and I fail to give thanks for Your blessings and for Your love. Today, help me to count those blessings, and let me give thanks to You, Father, for Your love, for Your grace, for Your blessings, and for Your Son. Amen

Celebration

This is the day which the LORD has made;
let us rejoice and be glad in it.

Psalm 118:24 NASB

A visit to the garden should be a cause for celebration. Do you feel like celebrating? Hopefully so. After all, this day—and every day—is a blessed gift from God.

What do you expect from the day ahead? Are you expecting God to do wonderful things, or are you living beneath a cloud of apprehension and doubt? The familiar words of Psalm 118:24 serve as a powerful reminder that each day is a cause for rejoicing.

Today, give thanks for the gift of life and for the One who created it. And then, use this day—a precious gift from the Father above—to serve your Savior faithfully, courageously, and joyfully.

More than half a century has passed,
and yet each spring, when I wander into the primrose wood,
I see the pale yellow blooms and smell their sweetest scent—
for a moment I am seven years old again
wandering in the fragrant wood.

Gertrude Jekyll

All our life is a celebration for us; we are convinced, in fact,
that God is always everywhere. We sing while we work . . .
we pray while we carry out all life's other occupations.

St. Clement of Alexandria

Rejoice always; pray without ceasing.

2 Thessalonians 5:16-17 NASB

Touch the earth, love the earth, honour the earth,
her plains, her valleys, her hills, and her seas;
rest your spirit in her solitary places.

Henry Beston

In all things of nature there is something of the marvelous.

Aristotle

I know nothing, except what everyone knows—
if there where God dances, I should dance.

W. H. Auden

Rejoice in the Lord always. I will say it again: Rejoice!

Philippians 4:4 HCSB

The early morning has gold in its mouth.

Ben Franklin

Earth gives life and seeks the man who walks gently upon it.

Hopi Legend

Some of us seem so anxious about avoiding hell
that we forget to celebrate our journey toward heaven.

Philip Yancey

At the dedication of the wall of Jerusalem, the Levites were sought out from where they lived and were brought to Jerusalem to celebrate joyfully the dedication with songs of thanksgiving and with the music of cymbals, harps and lyres.

Nehemiah 12:27 NIV

Where but in a garden do summer hours pass so quickly?

Anonymous

The poetry of the earth is never dead.

John Keats

Celebration is possible only through the deep realization that life and death are never found completely separate. Celebration can really come about only where fear and love, joy and sorrow, tear and smiles can exist together.

Henri Nouwen

David and the whole house of Israel were celebrating with all their might before the LORD, with songs and with harps, lyres, tambourines, sistrums and cymbals.

2 Samuel 6:5 NIV

In wilderness I sense the miracle of life,
and behind it our scientific accomplishments fade to trivia.

Charles A. Lindbergh

In a thousand unseen ways we have drawn shape and
strength from the land.

Lyndon B. Johnson

Consider every day that you are then for the first time—
as it were—beginning; and always act with
the same fervour as on the first day you began.

Anthony of Padua

So I recommend having fun, because there is nothing better for
people to do in this world than to eat, drink, and enjoy life.
That way they will experience some happiness along
with all the hard work God gives them.

Ecclesiastes 8:15 NLT

I am in love with the green earth.

Charles Lamb

All my life through, the new sights of nature
made me rejoice like a child.

Marie Curie

Each day, each moment is so pregnant
with eternity that if we "tune in" to it,
we can hardly contain the joy.

Gloria Gaither

Happy is he . . . whose hope is in the LORD his God.

Psalm 146:5 KJV

The only words that ever satisfied me as describing Nature are the terms used in fairy books, "charm," "spell," "enchantment."

G. K. Chesterton

The landscapes were like a violin bow that played upon my soul.

Stendhal

Every day should be a fantastic adventure for us because we're in the middle of God's unfolding plan for the ages.

John MacArthur

Rejoice, and be exceeding glad: for great is your reward in heaven . . . .

Matthew 5:12 KJV

A Gardener's Prayer

Lord, You have given me another day of life;
let me celebrate this day, and let me use it according to
Your plan. I praise You, Father, for my life and
for the friends and family members who make it rich.
Enable me to live each moment to the fullest
as I give thanks for Your creation, for Your love,
and for Your Son.
Amen

Abundance

And God is able to make all grace abound toward you,
that you, always having all sufficiency in all things,
may have an abundance for every good work.

2 Corinthians 9:8 NKJV

At harvest time, every gardener hopes for abundance. Sometimes the harvest is bountiful; sometimes it is not. But for Christians who place their lives in the hands of the One from Galilee, the spiritual harvest is always abundant.

Jesus offers life abundant and life eternal. Eternal life is the priceless possession of all who invite Christ into their hearts, but God's abundance is optional: He does not force it upon anyone.

The fullness of life in Christ is available to all who seek it and claim it. Count yourself among that number. Seek first the salvation that is available through a personal relationship with Jesus, and then claim the abundance that can—and should—be yours.

The creation of a thousand forests is in one acorn.

Ralph Waldo Emerson

Jesus intended for us to be overwhelmed by the blessings of regular days. He said it was the reason he had come: "I am come that they might have life, and that they might have it more abundantly."

Gloria Gaither

Each day is born anew for him who takes it rightly.

James Russell Lowell

My purpose is to give life in all its fullness.

John 10:10 HCSB

God is the giver, and we are the receivers.
And His richest gifts are bestowed not upon those
who do the greatest things, but upon those
who accept His abundance and His grace.

Hannah Whitall Smith

A garden is moved by influences you cannot see,
fully comprehend or control.
You are only part of the whole blooming thing.

Jamie Jobb

Nature's intelligence soars past our unused minds.

F. Lynne Bachleda

These things have I spoken unto you,
that my joy might remain in you, and that your joy might be full.

John 15:11 KJV

If you garden you think about gardens.
Ideas keep manifesting themselves,
they seep into your mind often
when you are nowhere near a garden.

Mirabel Osler

Jesus wants Life for us, Life with a capital L.

John Eldredge

A man's mind may be likened to a garden,
which may be intelligently cultivated or allowed to run wild;
but whether cultivated or neglected,
it must, and will, bring forth.

James Allen

Until now you have asked for nothing in My name.
Ask and you will receive, that your joy may be complete.

John 16:24 HCSB

Here is the great mystery of life and growth:
Everything is changing, growing, aiming at something,
but silently, unboastfully, taking its time.

Ruth Stout

God loves you and wants you to experience peace and life—
abundant and eternal.

Billy Graham

If you give, you will receive. Your gift will return to you
in full measure, pressed down, shaken together to make room
for more, and running over. Whatever measure you use in giving—
large or small—it will be used to measure what is given back to you.

Luke 6:38 NLT

We honor God by asking for great things when
they are a part of His promise. We dishonor Him and
cheat ourselves when we ask for molehills where
He has promised mountains.

Vance Havner

The more you learn what to do with yourself,
and the more you do for others,
the more you will learn to enjoy the abundant life.

William Boetcker

So many seeds—so little time.

Anonymous

Whoever has will be given more, and he will have an abundance.

Matthew 13:12 NIV

Though an old man, I am but a young gardener.

Thomas Jefferson

The universe is full of magical things
patiently waiting for our wits to grow sharper.

Eden Phillpotts

The proper function of mankind is to live not to exist.

Jack London

His master replied, "Well done, good and faithful servant!
You have been faithful with a few things;
I will put you in charge of many things.
Come and share your master's happiness!"

Matthew 25:21 NIV

If you want purpose and meaning and satisfaction and fulfillment and peace and hope and joy and abundant life that lasts forever, look to Jesus.

Anne Graham Lotz

Bloom where you're planted.

Mary Engelbreit

Instead of living a black-and-white existence, we'll be released into a Technicolor world of vibrancy and emotion when we more accurately reflect His nature to the world around us.

Bill Hybels

A pretentious, showy life is an empty life; a plain and simple life is a full life.

Proverbs 13:7 MSG

A Gardener's Prayer

Heavenly Father, thank You for the abundant life that is mine through Christ Jesus. You have given me a bountiful harvest—help me to be worthy of Your gifts. Guide me according to Your will, and help me follow in the footsteps of Your Son today and every day of my life.
Amen

And Finally . . .

We conclude with a bountiful harvest of quotations and Bible verses that are intended to enlighten those who garden and those who don't. Enjoy!

The best things that can come out of any garden are gifts for other people.

Jamie Jobb

If you want to be truly happy, you won't find it on an endless quest for more stuff. You'll find it in receiving God's generosity and the passing of that generosity along.

Bill Hybels

Every generous act and every perfect gift is from above, coming down from the Father of lights.

James 1:17 HCSB

Happiness grows at our own firesides,
and is not to be picked in strangers' gardens.

Douglas Jerrold

Happiness is the byproduct of a life that is lived
in the will of God. When we humbly serve others,
walk in God's path of holiness, and do what He tells us,
then we will enjoy happiness.

Warren Wiersbe

Delight thyself also in the LORD;
and he shall give thee the desires of thine heart.

Psalm 37:4 KJV

Most people don't see the sun, soil, bugs, seeds,
plants, moon, water, clouds,
and wind the way gardeners do.

Jamie Jobb

Distractions must be conquered or they will conquer us.
So let us cultivate simplicity; let us want fewer things;
let us walk in the Spirit; let us fill our minds
with the Word of God and our hearts with praise.

A. W. Tozer

A simple life in the Fear-of-God is better than
a rich life with a ton of headaches.

Proverbs 15:16 MSG

Confronted with the vision of a beautiful garden,
we see something beautiful about ourselves,
as a part of nature.

Jeff Cox

I may have tasted peace, but to believe that the God of heaven and earth calls me beautiful—well, I think I could rest in that. If I truly knew that He was smitten with me, maybe I could take a deep breath, square my shoulders, and go out to face the world with confidence.

Angela Thomas

. . . He [God] who began a good work in you
will carry it on to completion . . . .

Philippians 1:6 NIV

Keep close to Nature's heart and break clear away,
once in awhile, and climb a mountain or
spend a week in the woods. Wash your spirit clean.

John Muir

The movement from loneliness to solitude is
not a movement of a growing withdrawal from,
but rather a movement towards a deeper engagement
in the burning issues of our time.

Henri Nouwen

And he withdrew himself into the wilderness, and prayed.

Luke 5:16 KJV

Let the clean wind blow the cobwebs from your body.
Air is medicine.

Lillian Russell

People are funny. When they are young,
they will spend their health to get wealth.
Later, they will gladly pay all they have trying to get
their health back.

John Maxwell

Whatever you eat or drink or whatever you do,
you must do all for the glory of God.

1 Corinthians 10:31 NLT

Love the animals, love the plants, love everything.
If you love everything, you will perceive the divine mystery
in things. Once you perceive it,
you will begin to comprehend it better every day.
And you will come at last to love the whole world
with an all-embracing love.

Fyodor Dostoevsky

Life is immortal, love eternal; death is nothing
but a horizon, and a horizon is only the limit of our vision.

Corrie ten Boom

The best use of life is love.
The best expression of love is time.
The best time to love is now.

Rick Warren

The one who does not love does not know God, for God is love.

1 John 4:8 NASB

Mountains help us to regain that sense of freshness and wonder possessed by a child. They awaken us to a deeper reality hidden in the world around us, even in cities, far from the sight of the peaks themselves.

Edwin Bernbaum

A man who has lost his sense of wonder is a man dead.

William of St. Thierry

So don't lose a minute in building on what you've been given, complementing your basic faith with good character, spiritual understanding, alert discipline, passionate patience, reverent wonder, warm friendliness, and generous love, each dimension fitting into and developing the others.

2 Peter 1:5-7 MSG

Rivers have what man most respects and longs for in his own life and thought—a capacity for renewal and replenishment, continual energy, creativity, cleansing.

John M. Kauffmann

I wish I could make it all new again; I can't. But God can. "He restores my soul," wrote the shepherd. God doesn't reform; he restores. He doesn't camouflage the old; he restores the new. The Master Builder will pull out the original plan and restore it. He will restore the vigor, he will restore the energy. He will restore the hope. He will restore the soul.

Max Lucado

. . . the inward man is being renewed day by day.

2 Corinthians 4:16 NKJV

The present state of the world and the whole of life is diseased. If I were a doctor and were asked for my advice, I should reply: Create silence.

Søren Kierkegaard

Be still, and in the quiet moments, listen to the voice of your heavenly Father. His words can renew your spirit. No one knows you and your needs like He does.

Janet L. Weaver

My soul, wait silently for God alone,
For my expectation is from Him.

Psalm 62:5 NKJV

**God almighty
first planted a garden.
And, indeed, it is among
the purest of human pleasures.**

Francis Bacon